THE HEMINGWAY MONOLOGUES:

An Epic Drama
of Love, Genius and Eternity

THE HEMINGWAY MONOLOGUES:

An Epic Drama
Of Love, Genius and Eternity

PART FOUR: THE MAN-EATERS

A play in two acts

BRIAN GORDON SINCLAIR

The New
Atlantian Library

The New Atlantian Library
is an imprint of
ABSOLUTELY AMAZING Ebooks.

Published by Whiz Bang LLC, 926 Truman Avenue, Key West, Florida 33040, USA.

For information, contact:
Publisher@AbsolutelyAmazingEbooks.com

ISBN-13: 978-1945772658 (The New Atlantian Library)
ISBN-10: 1945772654

*THE MAN-EATERS is dedicated to
Tom Entwistle
(1970-2004)*

*Tom was the guide, not only through the
footsteps of the Spanish Civil War, but also into the
hearts of those who fought. His ashes lie now,
forever, on Hill 666 outside Madrid.*

PERFORMANCE RIGHTS

For the first time, with this publication, performances will be allowed by groups or individuals other than the author. No performance, other than by Brian Gordon Sinclair, may be given unless a license has been obtained from the author. No alterations may be made to the title or the text without prior written permission from the author.

The original production of *Part Four: The Man-Eaters* was multi-media and used a series of twin slide projections and a soundtrack. For performance purposes, the author, upon request, will provide a previous script with slide and sound effects indicated. The play, in its current form, has been rewritten to eliminate those effects. This revised script retains the original monologue while eliminating the need for costly production components and makes the show extremely portable for travel.

THE HEMINGWAY CHALLENGE

The author challenges any individual or theatrical company to present all seven Hemingway plays in one marathon event, either consecutively or as part of a single season. A single actor of immense stamina could be considered or multiple actors across the range of Hemingway's life.

For specific performance information, contact:
sinclair4814@rogers.com

For all other information, contact:
Publisher@AbsolutelyAmazingEbooks.com

Brian Gordon Sinclair as *Ernest Hemingway*

INTRODUCTION

The *Hemingway Monologues: An Epic Drama of Love, Genius and Eternity,* reads like an intimate memoir. A fascinating blend of fact and fiction, the

monologues reveal a tender, compassionate side of
Hemingway that most people have never encountered.
They can be enjoyed readily in performance or as a
good, absorbing read.

Originally intended to be one play detailing the life
of Ernest Hemingway, it became apparent that a life
that large could not be contained in one vessel. *The
Hemingway Monologues* evolved into a multi-play
series.

The Man-Eaters is the fourth play of the series.
Once again, a stage play illuminates both the writing
and the life of Ernest Hemingway in equal measures.
The Man-Eaters is a must see – must read production
for all lovers of Hemingway's books, for anyone
intrigued by his life and death. It is also a superb
introduction to Hemingway for the uninitiated.

The Hemingway Monologues consist of seven
plays. The first six plays present the Hemingway
chronology from birth to death. The seventh play is a
special edition compilation (See: "About the Author
and His Work" for a synopsis of each play):

1. *Part One: Sunrise*
2. *Part Two: The Lost Generation*
3. *Part Three: Death in the Afternoon*
4. ***Part Four: The Man-Eaters (this volume)***
5. *Part Five: The Death Factory*
6. *Part Six: Sunset (In Deadly Ernest)*
7. *Part Seven: Hemingway's HOT Havana*
(special compilation edition)

Brian Gordon Sinclair gives an intimate insight
into the circumstances which shaped the famed
author's life and inspired him in his writing.

The Man-Eaters debuted at the Hemingway Days
Festival in Key West, Florida in July of 2006 in support

of the Hemingway Collection at the Customs House Museum administered by the Key West Art and Historical Society. The final performance was attended by the Honourable Anthony Knill, Consul General of Canada.

Act I:
The first act begins with an exploration of Hemingway's relationship with Jane Mason in Cuba followed by a re-enactment of an African Safari as depicted in "The Short Happy Life of Francis Macomber". The monologue then examines life in Cuba under President Machado and the opposing revolutionary forces and concludes with Ernest defending his boat, Pilar, against pirates.

Act II:
In the second act, Hemingway travels to Spain and the Spanish civil war. He describes his role as a war correspondent and points out the various atrocities that take place on both sides of the war. Re-enactments of "Pilar's story" and "the death of El Sordo" from *For Whom the Bell Tolls* are included. The ending recreates Hemingway's address for the tenth anniversary of the Abraham Lincoln Brigade.

- Brian Gordon Sinclair

THE HEMINGWAY MONOLOGUES:

An Epic Drama
Of Love, Genius and Eternity

PART FOUR:
THE MAN-
EATERS

ACT ONE

Setting:
A table and chair sit stage left. On the table are the following: a full cocktail glass, a copy of For Whom the Bell Tolls, a model of the boat Pilar, a note of certification, paper and pencils, a typewriter and a Milton Wolff letter. Stage left of the table is a flag pole displaying the flag of the Spanish Republic. In front of the flag pole is a steamer trunk. On the trunk, hand-painted in red is the name Hemingway. Another table and chair sit stage right. On this table are the following: an ash-tray, another full cocktail glass, several books, a whiskey bottle, a red cloth filled with "Spanish Earth", a flashlight, a small stuffed lion,

wooden matches, a loaded blank pistol. In front of the stage right table is a wooden crate surrounded by appropriate sporting gear. Hidden behind the crate is a large rubber snake. Upstage centre is a coat rack with a bota, a crucifix and a Spanish shawl. Close by is a sledge hammer.

Music: The Ghost and the Darkness plays as the audience is seated.

<u>*AT RISE*</u>*:*
Lights fade to black.

Hemingway enters, sits at the stage left table, puts his glasses on and writes. As the music concludes, stage lights come up on the stage left side only. Hemingway interrupts his writing and speaks to the audience.

HEMINGWAY
Just a minute...

(He continues writing but reads as he writes.)

Kilimanjaro is a snow-covered mountain 19,710 feet high, and is said to be the highest mountain in Africa. Its western summit is called the Masai "Ngaje Ngai," the House of God. Close to the western summit there is the dried and frozen carcass of a leopard. No one has explained what the leopard was seeking at that altitude.

(He finishes writing and puts his pencil down.)

There!

(He rises and removes his glasses.)

Anyone can be a writer. All you have to do is sit down at a typewriter...and bleed.

Or you can go to Africa, get amoebic dysentery and do your bleeding there. That's what I did.

(Full lights.)

(He approaches the audience.)

My name is Ernest Hemingway and I am continuing my life in the original role of son-of-a-bitch, *san peur et sans reproche* ... without fear and without reproach.

There are many reasons why I went to Africa. One of them was a girl named Jane Mason. Jane was infatuated with me and she was obsessed with Africa or perhaps it was just that British hunter in Tanganyika. Whatever the reason, she convinced me to plan a safari ... with her ... and with my wife, Pauline. What a jungle that would have been. But Jane never made it and if you'll be patient I'll tell you why.

Jane was wealthy and she was beautiful, irresistible to men. She married even more wealth in the form of Grant Mason who was one of the founders of a little company called Pan American Airways.

Their Cuban home, Jaimanitas, was a pleasure palace. It was a Cole Porter world of cocktails and smoking and late night parties and fancy dress balls.
No matter what Jane wore, she always looked gorgeous and Grant...well Grant just looked silly most of the time. She was married to the wrong man and that was bad luck, for herself and for her friends.

The Hemingway Monologues

(He gets a drink from the stage right table.)

And Jane had friends everywhere. She had a passion for hunting and fishing and she sure could hold her booze. I admired that.

Salud!

(He drinks and returns the glass.)

She also collected writers as well as their books. I guess that's where I came in. With Pauline back in Key West and me writing alone in a two dollar a night room at the Hotel Ambos Mundos in Havana, I was a perfect target.

And then we targeted each other. Before lunch, we'd have plenty of daiquiris and then take off in her imported sports car.

(He moves the stage left chair forward and sits.)

It was a cross country chicken run. We had discovered the pure adrenaline rush of trying to scare the shit out of each other. The object was to see how long the passenger could sit there without shouting "Look out!" or "Stop!". The driver was free to leave the road and head out cross country. Ditches and thorn patches were legitimate hazards. So were cows, birds, trees and fallen logs. Oh, an ox cart gave you an extra point, but only if it was grazed, not smacked. Now, if you were sitting there in the passenger seat, you probably looked something like this.

(He leans back in the chair, gasps and looks terrified.)

Jane was a very careful driver. She always looked both ways before hitting something. When I drove, I cheated. I took my glasses off. Hell, I was so damned nearsighted that half the time I didn't know enough to be scared.

(He stands.)

My interest in Jane died the day she almost killed my children. She was taking Jack and Patrick back to Jaimanitas when she swerved to avoid a bus. At first, the boys thought she was playing our game but when the car started to roll over they knew it was for real. It rolled three times as they did a strange cartwheel, their hands pressed forcibly against the roof of the car which finally buckled. The door was jammed but they managed to scramble out the window. It was not fatal, but it could have been.

The next day, Jane fell off her balcony at Jaimanitas. I joked about it and told everyone that she had fallen for me ... but it wasn't funny. Her back was broken and so was our relationship. Someone said that it was no accident, that Jane had gone a little crazy. Whatever it was, she was spending too much time inside her head and that was a bad neighbourhood. That's why I went to Africa without her.

Oh, there is one other thing to clear up. Some people say I had sex with Jane Mason. Other people say I did not have sex with Jane Mason. Are you familiar with the expression, "kiss and tell"? Well, here's the truth ... Yes! ... Yes, I kissed Jane Mason.

(He starts to walk away and stops.)

And no, I will not tell you what happened that time she climbed in the balcony of my room at the Hotel Ambos Mundos and found me lying there with a great big ... Never you mind what she found!

(He returns the stage left chair.)

Another reason I went to Africa was the Man-Eating Lions of Tsavo. As a child, I had read that book and I spent many long hours dreaming in the African section of the Field Museum in Chicago. In those days, security was pretty lax and if I crouched behind a big stone pillar, I could stay after hours and dream as long as I wanted. The only problem was getting home late. My sisters covered for me while I hid out under the neighbour's porch until I could sneak safely into the house. That neighbour knew I was there and, every time, she left a huge piece of fresh baked apple pie right beside the porch. Africa and apple pie ... now that was a deal.

It wasn't until 1928, when I came home for my father's funeral, that I actually saw the Man-Eating Lions of Tsavo. I went to the museum because I was so damn depressed I had to get out of the house.

Back in 1898, near the Tsavo River in East Africa, two large male lions killed and ate 140 railway workers. It was Col. John Patterson who finally brought the lions down but it took him nine months to do it.

The first lion measured nine feet eight inches from nose to tail and it took eight men to carry the carcass back to camp. I guess dining on all those tasty rail workers can tend to make a lion gain a few pounds.

Four years before I saw them, the man-eaters arrived at the museum ... as rugs. By the time I saw them, they were stuffed and restored, an absolute marvel of taxidermy. As I stared at them, I remembered that child who, years ago, had dreamed of being an African warrior or a great hunter and I knew I had to go. But I didn't want mangy, old carpets. I wanted a magnificent, full maned beast.

In 1934, I got my wish. And I got two other things with it, amoebic dysentery and a damn fine lion story. I might as well give you the bad news first.

When I arrived in Africa, I was a bit of a smart-ass so I asked our guide, Philip "Pop" Percival if there were any cannibals. I told him it was important to know because I didn't want to end up in hot water. But that's exactly what happened.

At first, I thought I was just a jerk with a belly-ache but it was amoebic dysentery, sometimes known as AD or to those in the know as DF, diarrhea forever.

For a while, I thought I could continue hunting but when you have to go every five minutes, it's hard to last long enough to shoot anything.

(He mimes lowering his pants beside the wooden crate.)

I tried to go in the three-foot grass ... tall enough to squat in without showing my bare behind and short enough to watch for lions. But I forgot something ... as I reached for some grass to clean myself I felt something soft.

(He reaches behind the wooden crate and picks up the prop snake.)

Oh shit! I forgot about snakes.

There is nothing more ridiculous than a man with his pants down around his ankles, a snake in his hand, shouting and dancing, until he remembers what he is holding. Jesus!

(He tosses the snake into the audience.)

Eventually, I ended up in bed, fully injected with emetine, having been flown four hundred miles to a hospital in Nairobi. The symptoms of AD run from weakly insidious through spectacular to phenomenal. Phenomenal includes what they call explosive diarrhea. I believe the record is held by a Mr. McDonald with 232 movements in twenty-four hours, although many old AD men claim the McDonald record was never properly handled ... I mean audited.

I think we'll close the lid on that one and move on to the lion story.

There are two ways to murder a lion. One is to shoot him from a motor car; the other is to shoot him at night with a flashlight from a platform as he comes to feed on the bait left out by the tourist. These two ways to murder a lion rank, as sport, with dynamiting trout or harpooning swordfish. Yet many men return home and think of themselves as sportsmen and big game hunters, having killed lions from a motor car or a platform.

Francis Macomber could have been such a man but you can judge for yourself as I tell you the story of his short, happy life and I'll make it real simple for you. Grant Mason is Frances and Jane Mason is his wife, Margot Macomber.

There is an old Somali proverb that says a brave man is always frightened three times by a lion: when he first sees his track, when he first hears him roar and when he first confronts him.

Francis Macomber had wakened the night before and heard the lion roaring. It was a deep sound that made him seem just outside the tent and when Francis heard it, he was afraid.

The lion roared again. It was a deep-chested vibration that seemed to shake the air...and what was left of Macomber's nerves.

That morning, he set out with Margot and their guide, Robert Wilson. After a while, they saw the birds dropping. Wilson said it meant the old boy has left his kill. Above the trees, vultures circled and plummeted down.

"There he is. Ahead and to the right. Get out and take him. He's a marvelous lion."

The lion looked huge, silhouetted on the rise of bank in the gray morning light. But Macomber was afraid. He wanted to shoot from the car.

"You don't shoot them from cars," hissed Wilson.

The lion watched and was not afraid.

Bang!

Then he felt the slam of a .30-06 220 grain solid bullet that hit his flank and ripped in a sudden hot scalding nausea through his stomach. Macomber had gut shot him.

Bang!

The next bullet hit his lower ribs and ripped on through, the blood hot and frothy in his mouth and he galloped toward the high grass where he could crouch and not be seen, where he could make a rush and get the man who held the cracking thing.

Macomber's hands were shaking. It was almost impossible for him to make his legs move and he was sick to his stomach. The lion was in a bad place. You wouldn't see him until you were on him. Macomber could see the blood, dark red on the short grass and he did not want to go in there. He was so scared that he was sweating and trembling and all he wanted to do was leave.

Thirty-five yards into the grass the big lion lay flattened out along the ground. His ears were back and his only movement was a slight twitching up and down of his long, black-tufted tail. He was sick with the wound through his full belly and with the wound through his lungs that brought a thin foamy red to his mouth. His big, yellow eyes, narrowed with hate, looked straight ahead, only blinking when the pain came as he breathed, and his claws dug in the soft baked earth. All of him, pain, sickness, hatred and all of his remaining strength, was tightening into one absolute concentration for a rush. As he heard their voices, his tail stiffened and as they came into the edge of the grass, he made a coughing grunt and charged.

Macomber heard the blood-choked grunt, and he saw the swishing rush in the grass. The next thing he knew he was running, running wildly, in panic in the open, running toward the stream.

There were two shots. He turned and saw the lion, horrible-looking now, his head half gone, crawling toward Wilson.

There was another shot. Then the crawling, heavy yellow bulk of the lion stiffened and the huge, mutilated head slid forward.

Two black men and the white hunter looked at Macomber with contempt. His wife did not even look at him. He had proved himself a coward.

Margot walked over to Robert Wilson and she kissed him ... and that night she had sex with him.

Macomber knew she was through with him but suddenly none of it seemed important anymore. He knew she wouldn't leave. He had too much money.

The next day they went out after buffalo. They killed three, or so they thought until a bearer ran up and told them that the first bull had gone off into the bush, just like the lion. Macomber expected the feeling he'd had about the lion to come back but it didn't. For the first time in his life he felt wholly without fear. He knew that he would never be afraid of anything again. He felt absolutely different.

The Hemingway Monologues

Margot said nothing but eyed him strangely. Francis Macomber had come of age. He had stopped being a scared little boy. No more fear, no more cuckoldry. But now, suddenly, Margot was very afraid ... of something.

Macomber felt his heart pounding and his mouth was dry again, but this time it was excitement, not fear. He saw the bull coming out of the bush, nose out, mouth tight closed, blood dripping, massive head straight out, coming in a charge, his little pig eyes all bloodshot.

Macomber fired and fragments like slate burst from the huge horns.

Aiming carefully, he fired again with the buffalo's huge bulk almost on him and his rifle almost level with the on-coming head and he could see the little wicked eyes and the head started to lower and ... suddenly there was another shot, and he felt a sudden white-hot blinding flash explode inside his head...and that was all he ever felt.

Mrs. Macomber, from the car, had shot at the buffalo with the 6.5 Mannlicher as it seemed about to gore Francis and had hit her husband about two inches up and a little to one side of the base of his skull. Francis Macomber lay now, face down, not two yards from where the buffalo lay, both very, very dead.

By now, you might realize that I've lied to you. At the moment of death, Margot was really my wife and I was Francis Macomber. Every time I felt sorry for myself, I saw Pauline as the enemy, like my mother. Margot had married a man she could handle but what I saw was my mother controlling my father. She was another man-eater. It wasn't Margot who shot me and it was not Jane

Mason. It was Pauline. She was too rich, I was too spoiled and she dulled the edge of my talent.

(He takes a drink stage left.)

Now if you believe all that then you better listen to this one.

(He takes the stage right chair, places it backwards and sits.)

There was this Easterner who came to me one day and asked me to help him shoot a grizzly. "It's all my wife wants," he said. "Night and day she's after me, and since we're just married, I'd like to please her." Hell, I say, the grizzly is the hardest of all bears to shoot, the toughest and the smartest. I haven't shot a grizzly in eight years.

Well, I'm out with this husband and wife one day, and we're stalking a moose for food when there's a sound in the brush and three grizzlies appear. They are gargantuan sons-of-bitches. I tell the wife to get behind me because there's no time to get to cover.
The husband, who is terrified, has already run for cover and is out of the action. Now, listen, a grizzly will drop when he's hit but he'll usually recover and charge and he won't drop again until he's dead. That's what makes them so damn dangerous. The nearest grizzly, an eight-hundred pounder, takes one look at us and charges straight on. I drop him with a neck shot and as he starts to get up, I drill him in the shoulder for keeps.

The second grizzly charges while I'm reloading and I empty both shells into him practically point-blank. He's dead on arrival. Now the third grizzly, who's cased the fate of his buddies and wants no part of it, turns and starts up the hill and I have to peg him four times before I put him away for good. Then, the new wife emerges from the shadow of my behind and she says to me, "My mouth is dry. Please cover me while I go to the stream to get a drink." And that's all she ever said about the entire episode. And people want to know if Margot Macomber was drawn from real life!

(He stands.)

All of these things have some truth but I never wrote about any one person. They were composites, a mixture of a lot of things and that made for a new character. Ladies and gentlemen, the truth is in the writing. Enjoy it and for Chris'sake, let your own imagination do some of the work.
Speaking of imagination, no safari would be complete without a photograph of the hunter and his trophy.

(He picks up the stuffed lion.)

So let's get a good shot of yours truly with this magnificent fully-manned beast.

(He places the lion on the floor, puts his foot on it and poses.)
Shoot!

There...and don't ever think that the creatures of the jungle are not dangerous. You never know when they'll go right for your throat, like this.

(He tosses the toy lion into the audience and growls.)

(He returns the chair.)

By the way, Francis Macomber was the name of a student who went to the same high school I did in Oak Park. I hardly knew him but I thought it was a swell name.

(He picks up the model of the Pilar.)

It wasn't long before the thrill of the safari was replaced by the thrill of my new boat, the *Pilar*. Aside from being one fine fishing machine, the *Pilar* could get me away from Pauline and into Havana harbor in record time.

Some people say I liked Cuba and the fishing because it gave me a chance to prove my manhood. They're absolutely right. Every morning I got up and said, "Well, I think I'll go out and prove my manhood today."

(He returns the Pilar.)

I love Havana. Most of all, I love waking in the morning to the sun rising beside the Moro Castle. I love hearing the clatter of the ice wagons on cobblestone streets as they drip their liquid gold. The children run behind them trying to catch a frozen diamond. The peasants are waking in the streets, merchants are sweeping in front of their shops and the lottery sellers are setting up their tables. The fat whore has gone home. The stringy whore is just finishing up but will be on her way soon. All in all, it is a quiet, drowsy morning in Havana.

Then, over at the cemetery, a huge explosion. Jesus, gravestones were flying up into the air. To find out why, you had to ask Alphonso. But first, you got the speech; everybody got the speech.

"I am a member of the ABC's", he said. "It is a very powerful and secret organization. If you do not do what we tell you, we will kill you. If we tell you to throw a bomb at your own house and you do not do it, we will shoot you. That is why we are so powerful."

"Now," he said, "I will tell you about the explosion. There was this general who ordered his men to shoot one of our ABC's. The next day, we discovered he had ordered a pair of boots from a factory, so we made a package with a bomb inside. A flashlight battery was fixed so the wires would touch when the package was opened. Then I intercepted the messenger from the factory and told him I was from the general. I paid him the thirty dollars and took our package to the hotel clerk. 'These are the boots for the general.' The bellboy took the package up to the general's room and a few minutes afterward the whole building shook with a great big bang! They found the general splattered all over the ceiling.

"Then," Alphonso said, "the ABC's got really busy. President Machado was going to have a big military funeral for the general and all the big shots would be there. This was a chance to really clean up. That night we dug a tunnel in the cemetery near the open grave for the general. We filled it with hundreds of pounds of dynamite and set a clock so it would go off at the time of the funeral. But...there are two cemeteries close to each other and, at the last minute, Machado decided to have the general buried in the other cemetery. Well, that spoiled everything. As Machado and his officers were standing around the grave of the general, waiting for the soldiers to shoot their rifles over the coffin, they heard this huge explosion.

And that is why the gravestones went flying up into the air at the other cemetery. It was the wrong damn cemetery."

I was curious, so I asked, "Why do Cubans have revolutions all the time?"

"It's simple," he said. "Our government officials get too rich robbing from the poor. We have to throw them out of office and get new ones."

"But you never keep the new ones."

"Of course not, because soon they start to rob from the poor, just like the old ones."

"Well, aren't there any honest politicians?"

"Oh, maybe at first" he said, "before they learn how to rob, but with power, they all turn crooked."

"Then what's the use?"

Alphonso looked me straight in the eye and said, "Look, I know we cannot govern but we sure can revolt ... and all these explosions, they are the music of the revolution.

Yes, I loved Havana and Havana loved me, especially the pirates.

The word "pirate" still strikes fear into the heart of every man at sea. Pirates exist and there are more of them in depression times. In Havana, at first, I was considered one of the wealthy yacht club set and my boat, the *Pilar*, had caught the eye of many a pirate since her first visit. There was no doubt that she seemed fair game to the rough crowd of Havana harbor.

...Fair game to all those bum boatmen and thieves who prowled the waterfront in their row boats and skiffs. Some of them even had small motor launches and would try for an even bigger prize, an unsuspecting freighter and its crew. These water pirates were not averse to murder.

They were also famous for their pride and skill. Last year they held a competition out at the race track. The thief who won demonstrated that he was so good that he could steal the shoes off a horse, while it was still racing.

It wasn't long before the word was out. "Get the *Pilar!*" But the word was so far out, that some of my friends heard it and tipped me off. For the next few nights, I kept watch on board. After rowing out with a friend, I had the friend row back again with a large sack in the stern. It resembled a figure hunched over and going ashore with him. And then I waited, patiently, inside the cabin, listening...Shhh! Can you hear that? It was the sound I was waiting for, the gentle dip-dip of muffled oars approaching. Soon, a small boat came alongside in absolute silence. For a moment, all was still. Suddenly, a dark figure rose up on the deck, fully silhouetted against the background of café lights from the shore.

(He picks up the pistol.)

The last thing he heard was the faint click of my Colt .45 as my thumb pulled back the hammer and...

(Hemingway fires the pistol, puts it down and picks up a flashlight.)

There was a splash as the figure fell overboard. I got my flashlight and shone it over the surface of the water. Nothing ... only a small empty boat drifting slowly out to sea."

After that, the word went out again, "Stay away from Hemingway's boat."

(Blackout)

END of ACT I: INTERMISSION

THE HEMINGWAY MONOLOGUES:

An Epic Drama
Of Love, Genius and Eternity

PART FOUR:
THE MAN-
EATERS

ACT TWO

AT RISE:

Music: Jarama Valley plays while the audience takes their seats.

When the houselights go out, Hemingway enters and sits in a chair centre stage. He is wrapped in a quilt of Spanish design and is holding a manuscript.

As the lights come up, Hemingway whistles softly and makes an explosive sound. It is the sound of a bomb.

The Hemingway Monologues

HEMINGWAY
They say you never hear the one that hits you. That's true of bullets, because, if you hear them, they are already past. I heard the last shell that hit the hotel this morning. I heard it come in with a whistling incoming roar like a subway train.

But I felt safe wrapped in this old Spanish quilt. It's a strong quilt, strong enough to protect me and strong enough to protect this manuscript. Every day, I would come back and find the quilt and the manuscript safe under the mattress where I left them and I was pleased.

(He folds the manuscript in the quilt and places it stage right. He picks up a folded red cloth.)

Wrapped in this other cloth is something even more special than my manuscript.

(He kneels, unwraps the cloth and places it on the floor .)

This is the earth, the Spanish Earth and it is stained with the blood of the Spanish people, with the blood of Lorca and with the blood of brothers.

(He crosses himself and rises.)

It has been going on now in Spain, all day and all night long, for over a year and a half. So you are tired of it. Even the word doesn't mean anything anymore. War is not a word that frightens people any longer. They are getting used to it now.

But not in Madrid. In Madrid, things changed, for the worse. The streets were full of the usual Sunday crowds, cheerful, optimistic, shopping for clothing and jewelry, lined up at the sand-bagged cinemas ... and then the shells came.

(He claps his hands.)

They came with a sudden flash. That morning, twenty-two shells came into Madrid.

They killed an old woman returning home from market, dropping her in a huddled black heap of clothing, with one leg, suddenly detached, whirling against the wall of an adjoining house.

They killed three people in another square where a shell left them buried in dust and rubble.

(He returns the chair stage right.)

A motor car coming along the street swerved and stopped suddenly. The driver lurched out with his scalp hanging down over his eyes and sat down on the sidewalk, his hand against his face, the blood running down over his lips and chin.

The shelling that killed those Sunday promenaders was not military. It was annihilation of the innocent. The man-eaters were eating their prey and Franco and Mussolini and Hitler were very hungry.

Some of the men, young and old, died well in battle. Like the boy who was shot through the head. And the man who was hit in the hand. He bandaged that wound, and then was killed by a bullet in the back. There was nothing very odd nor very extraordinary about any of these wounds; and in this last year, I saw many people that I knew die in the same way.

There were three Italian soldiers who came to Spain to die but didn't have very good luck at it. The first man was hit by high explosives. Only pieces of him remain. The second man had no feet to his legs and the third man was without his head. Another man, dead from the same shell, looks all right. There's nothing very startling about him; but he is quite dead.

One man was hit by a light bomb dropped from a pursuit plane. If you could see him, you'd be impressed, if you're not used to a battle-field. But I've seen others just as bad or worse. I remember him quite well because when I turned what was left of him over, I found a letter from his wife. In it, she wrote that she cried every night because he was not there ... and now he will never be there, ever again.

This is what happens to the men sent to die in a fascist invasion of a democratic country.

The men who are defending that country against the Moors, the Italians and the Germans, die in the same ugly way. But they die knowing why they die; they die fighting for you now; knowing that unless they beat the fascists now, you will have to fight them later. Many of them came a long way to die in Spain and none of them got more than fifty cents a day for it. The men of the International Brigades were not soldiers of fortune or adventurers. They were just men who thought long and hard about what was right. No one sent them. They came to Spain to fight fascism because they saw, long before the diplomats, how dangerous it was.

The so-called democratic countries allowed Spain to be over-run by the fascists. They refused to allow the legal Spanish republican government to buy arms to fight not only a military uprising but also a fascist invasion. Meanwhile, Italy sent another 50,000 troops. Germany delivered four hundred new warplanes and supplied three brigades with both artillery and tanks. No matter what excuses the democratic countries give, history will label their actions as criminal stupidity. But you people who don't have to go hungry or fight and die, you don't want to hear about it. Well perhaps this story will make it seem a little more real. Because this story is what will happen to our boys after the next war ... and this story is what will happen to our boys after every war that will ever happen.

I was hired by the North American Newspaper Alliance to go to Spain and report on the war. To be a war correspondent is incredibly important. It's my job to let the people of America know what is happening to their soldiers, their volunteers, to their children and no one else can tell them. That is my job, to send home as much of the truth as I possibly can.

Speaking of truth, it was Geothe who said, "Be bold and mighty forces will come your way." Obviously he wasn't referring to Franklin Delano Roosevelt because he just sat there on his big fat mighty while Hitler and Mussolini sent their forces to Franco and the Nationalists. Roosevelt said he wanted to stay away from the Spanish Civil War because he was too busy cleaning up Herbert Hoover's mess. Hell, the only American president who didn't blame the previous administration for his problems was George Washington.

Anyway, you already know what I thought of Roosevelt after the '35 hurricane in the Florida Keys. That's where he abandoned hundreds of World War I veterans and left them there to drown.

Not everything was a Spanish tragedy. In a strange way, I enjoyed all this. I even thrived on it. Somehow, I get more cheerful the worse things go. This isn't bragging. I wasn't always that way. I think it's part of growing up. You get to be one way or another and I turned out to be one of the cheerful bastards.

This cheerfulness though was put to the test by the chauffeurs of Madrid.

In Spain, we got around by car and chauffeur, arranged by the Republican government. We went through a lot of chauffeurs. The first one was named Tomas. He was four feet eleven inches high and looked like a particularly unattractive dwarf out of a *Velázquez* painting who was squeezed into a pair of blue dungarees. He had several front teeth missing and reeked of Scotch whiskey. Not your average good looking Spaniard.

Tomas had a problem with steering wheels. He rarely used them. On the way into Madrid, he abandoned the wheel, clapped me on the back and shouted, "Long live Madrid!" simultaneously scaring the hell out of a lorry full of troops that he ran off the road and into the ditch. He told me that he was a man of sentiment. I told him to keep his goddamn sentimental hands on the goddamn steering wheel.

The next day three rebel planes bombed us. Nothing hit us but Tomas started shaking and he got out of there as fast as possible.

Next morning, strangely, he couldn't get the car to start. In fact, from then on, no matter how well the car had run coming home, it would not start in the morning. Finally, we sent him home to Valencia and asked the press department if they could send us someone just a little braver.

(He picks up a note stage left.)

So they sent us one with a note actually certifying him as the bravest chauffeur in the whole department. I saw the note but I never saw him. He was given a car with forty liters of very hard to obtain petrol and was told to check in at the hotel at seven-thirty to see if there were any new orders. He never showed up. He had left that same morning for Valencia with the car and the forty liters of petrol. He's in jail in Valencia now and I hope he likes it there. Maybe Tomas will come to visit him.

(Return the note.)

Next we got David, an Anarchist boy from a little town near Toledo. He used language that was so foul, it changed my whole conception of profanity.

David was absolutely brave but he had one real defect as a chauffeur. He couldn't drive a car ... but he could sneak along, in second gear and hit practically no one in the streets, due to his clearing a swathe ahead of him with his foul vocabulary.

We solved the problem. We drove David ourselves. He liked this. It gave him a chance to really work with his vocabulary.

David liked the war and after watching his first battle, which seemed to him like a beautiful fireworks show, he shouted, "That's war. That's really war. Listen to that unspeakable, unmentionable noise."

(He sits at the stage left table.)

I had better things to do, so I went back to the Hotel Florida to write some dispatches. I sent David over to a place near the *Plaza Mayor* to get some petrol. I was still working later when there was a knock at the door. It was David. His face was pale and his lips were trembling.

"The car," he said, "the car was full of blood." A shell had hit a line of women waiting to buy food. It killed seven of them and David took another three to the hospital. That's why the car was full of blood. He didn't even know there were such things.

(He stands.)

"Listen, David," I said. "You're a brave boy. You must remember that. But all day you have been brave about noises. What you see now is what those noises do."

He never did learn to drive a car ... and he never thought that war was quite as beautiful again.

Finally we got Hipolito. Hipolito is the point of this story. He was carved out of a granite block and he had an automatic pistol so big it came halfway down his leg ... at least, I think it was a pistol. He always said "*Salud*," he knew motors, he could drive and if you told him to show up at six a.m., he was there ten minutes before six.

He made you realize why Franco never took Madrid when he had the chance. Hipolito and the others like him would have fought from street to street, and house to house, as long as any one of them was left alive. They are tough and they are efficient. They are the Spaniards that once conquered the Western World ... and they are not afraid to die.

One day, we had over 300 shells come into Madrid but Hipolito didn't care. He insisted on driving us to the *Hotel Gran Via* for lunch "Don't worry,' he said, "They're eating their lunch too."
Food was scarce, but we managed a meager meal of bean soup, paper thin sliced sausage and an orange while Hipolito waited in the car.

Outside there was an explosion. I ran out and around the corner to the car. But it was too late. The car was covered with dust and rubble. They got Hipolito. He was lying there with his head back in the driver's seat. I had grown very fond of him but as I leaned over, I heard a strange sound ... Snoring!

The son-of-a-bitch was asleep. He had nerves like steel, and slept right through the whole damn thing.

"*Que va, hombre,*" he said. "I always sleep a little after lunch if I have time."

The man was absolutely indestructible.

When I left Madrid, I tried to give him some money but he wouldn't take it. He felt we'd had a good time and settled for a drink at Chicote's Bar.

You can bet on Franco, or Mussolini, or Hitler, if you want. But my money goes on Hipolito.

Something I would not bet on though is the purity or the righteousness of either side in the civil war. Spain was a carnival of treachery and rottenness and any government and any revolution would twist the nation to their point of view and they would sacrifice anyone who gets in the way.

(He picks up For Whom the Bell Tolls stage left.)

That's what happened in the story told by Pilar in *For Whom the Bell Tolls*. In the beginning, it was not a fight for democracy against fascism. It was a revolution, a revolution against the church, against the factories and against the land barons. The Spanish workers were tired of being beaten down and they rose up against it.

But sometimes, the desire for revenge is so strong that the horror is past all logic. The world goes mad ... and you can lose your faith in those dark moments that are beyond comprehension.

Pilar, the woman who tells this story, was a republican and she was the leader of a band of Guerillas in the mountains. Pilar was so ugly that she was beautiful. Her husband, Pablo, was ugly too, and he stayed that way.

This is Pilar's story.

(He reads.)

It was early in the morning when the *civiles* surrendered at the barracks. Pablo had surrounded it in the dark, cut the telephone wires, placed dynamite under one wall and called on the *guardia civil* to surrender. They would not. At daylight, he blew the wall open. Two *civiles* were killed. Four were wounded and four surrendered.

There was a shout from within the smoke not to fire any more and out came the four *civiles* with their hands up. Inside the wounded were groaning and crying out. Pablo stood the four against the wall and went in to finish the others.

(He closes and returns the book.)

When he came out there was no more crying. In his hand was a Mauser pistol and it is an ugly pistol.

The four *civiles* knelt with their heads against the wall. Pablo passed behind them and shot each in turn in the back of the head.

No one came to help. They couldn't, they were all locked in the city hall. The night before, Pablo seized them in their homes, twenty of them, all fascists...and all to be killed.

On three sides of the plaza is arcade but on the fourth side is the edge of a high cliff and far below, the river. It is three hundred feet down to the river.

Pablo is very intelligent and very brutal. He blocked the entrances to the streets leading to the city hall and remained inside with the prisoners. Under the barrel of Pablo's shotgun, the priest administered the sacraments. Outside, the townspeople formed two lines from the door clear across the plaza to the edge of the cliff. They formed a gauntlet, armed with flails and hammers and pitchforks. Some had sickles and reaping hooks.

The lines were quiet and it was a clear day. You could hear the water running from the brass pipe in the mouth of the lion and falling into the bowl of the fountain.

At the front of the line the republican peasants were nervous. They wondered if there would be women to kill...

(He picks up the hammer.)

...and they wondered if one blow with this was enough to kill a man...or would it take several?

If you have not seen the day of revolution in a small town where all know all in the town and always have known all, you have seen nothing.

(He returns the hammer.)

It was done this way for two reasons: to save bullets and to have each man share in the responsibility.

They stood sweating in the sun waiting for it to commence. The fascists needed time to confess their sins. While they were waiting, someone threw his hat off the cliff by the river. It sailed far out into space, getting smaller and smaller, down and down into the river.

Here comes the first one. It was the Mayor, Don Benito Garcia. He walked slowly but nothing happened. He passed two men, four men eight men, ten men, still nothing happened. Then someone cried out, "What's the matter, cowards?" A man raised his flail high and struck Don Benito on the head. He struck again and then they all beat him until he fell. With his face in the dust they dragged him to the edge of the cliff and threw him over and he sailed, just like the hat, down and down into the river.

The feed store owner was next but he was trembling so much he couldn't walk so one of the drunkards poked him forward with a pitchfork until those at the end of the line picked him up and swung him over the cliff.

Inside, they continued praying. Don Ricardo kissed a crucifix and stepped outside. He looked at the double line of peasants and spat on the ground, "Down with your unnamable Republic. I obscenity in the milk of your fathers." Before this, there was no great taste for blood. Now they were angry, so they clubbed him to death and then they chopped him up with reaping hooks and sickles. This time, when they threw him over the cliff there was blood on their hands.

The next man stepped out, took one look, and tried to run back to the door. What he ran into was Pablo's shotgun. He threw himself down on the ground and began crying. You could still hear him crying as his body floated down through the air.

Now it was Don Guillarmo's turn. Don Guillermo was the merchant who had sold them their flails, who had always helped them but that didn't matter now. Cruelty and drunkenness had taken over. As he walked forward, a woman started to scream. It was his wife. "Wait, Guillermo," she said, "wait and I will be with thee." Then some drunkard laughed and imitated her voice. With tears running down his cheeks, Don Guillermo rushed towards the man. The man hit him hard across the face. They all hit him and then the drunkard jumped on his back and beat him to death with a bottle. All the time they shouted, *"Viva la Anarquia. Viva la Libertad."* They should have shouted, "Long live drunkenness."

The last man to be pushed out by Pablo was Don Anastasio. Don Anastasio was the fattest man in town. With his fat neck bulging and his bald head shining in the sun, he stumbled and fell. The lines broke and the men rushed in and piled on top of him. They beat his head against the stone again and again, until he was dead. This time they didn't even throw him over the cliff, they just left him there. They wanted inside the city hall. They wanted the rest of them. That's when the mob charged the door and began pounding.
Bang! Bang! Bang!

Inside, the remaining fascists continued to pray. Pablo and his men turned over two tables and some benches and made a barricade for themselves in the corner of the room. One of the men unlocked the door and ducked behind it as the mob rushed in. Suddenly, the hall was full of men clubbing and stabbing and shouting and the prisoners were screaming, screaming the way horses scream in a fire. They held the priest and hacked at him with reaping hooks. Then two men held his robes as another chopped into his back with a sickle. Finally, when the room smelled of urine and vomit and blood, the screaming ended.

(He picks up a bottle and matches and sits in the stage right chair.)

Outside, a man with a whiskey bottle saw Don Anastasio lying face down with his blood staining the ground. He leaned over and poured whiskey onto the head of Don Anastasio and onto his clothes, and then he took a matchbox out of his pocket and lit several matches, trying to make a fire. But the wind was blowing hard and it blew the matches out, so he sat there shaking his head and drinking out of the bottle and every once in a while, leaning over and patting the shoulders of the dead body. Again, he poured whiskey and lit a match. Pouring and lighting and pouring and lighting and then the wind stopped. The match caught and a blue flame began to run up the back of Don Anastasio and onto his neck. The drunkard leaned back. "They're burning the dead," he said. "They're burning the dead."

(He stands.)

That was the end of the killing of the fascists in that town.

(He returns the bottle and matches to the table.)

I could not have told this story during the war. Even later, some of the American volunteers in the Abraham Lincoln Brigade felt that I had betrayed the cause of the republic, because I had shown them at their worst.

(He picks up For Whom the Bell Tolls.)

What they did not mention was when I showed them at their best. When I told the story of the death of El Sordo, the guerilla leader, that was my attempt to show the courage of a group of brave republicans, men who would not surrender.

(He reads.)

El Sordo was making his fight on a hilltop. He knew that as long as his ammunition and grenades held out they could not move him. Not until the planes came.

He knew they would die as soon as a mortar came up, but when he thought of the planes, he felt as naked on the hilltop as though all of his clothing and even his skin had been removed.

Lying behind his dead horse, Sordo looked up at the bright, high, blue early summer sky. He was fifty-two years old and he was sure this was the last time he would see that sky.

(He puts the book down.)

Then he felt a touch on his shoulder. He turned and saw the gray, fear-drained face of Joaquin and he looked where the boy was pointing and saw the three planes coming. The planes were coming on steadily. They were in echelon and each second they grew larger and their noise was greater.

Sordo put the gun on the shoulder of the boy and told him not to move. The three legs of the tripod were dangling down the boy's back and the muzzle of the gun was shaking from the jerking of his body. He couldn't control it. All he could do was pray. "Hail Mary full of grace, the Lord is with thee; Blessed art thou..."

Then there were hammering explosions and his ears were deafened and his back was burning and then there came, through the hammering, the whistle of the air splitting ... and then the earth rolled under his knees and waved up to hit him in the face. Dirt and bits of rock were falling all over. A body was lying on him and the gun was lying on him. But he was not dead, not yet ... and then it came again...

...and the earth lurched under his belly and one side of the hilltop rose into the air and then fell slowly over him.

The planes came back three times and bombed the hilltop but no one on the hilltop knew it. The planes machine-gunned the hilltop and then they went away...into the sky.

Into this confusion, a fascist lieutenant threw four grenades, but no one was alive on the hilltop except the boy who was unconscious under the dead body of his comrade. The lieutenant, a good catholic, made the sign of the cross. Then he shot Joaquin in the back of the head. Next, he ordered his men to cut off the head of El Sordo. He ordered his men to cut off all their heads. As they did this, he did not watch. He looked away and said, "Que cosa mas mala es la guerra. What a bad thing war is."

(He picks up For Whom the Bell Tolls again.)

When I write, I try to tell the truth, all sides of it and I never forgot for a moment the horror that was approaching. To open the door for Hitler would mean the death of millions. The death of El Sordo was one of the first.

(He returns the book, picks up the Wolff letter and reads.)

Milton Wolff was the last commander of the Lincoln Brigade. Milt was a good man but he said some pretty nasty things about me. Like these:

"Ernest Hemingway is toadying to the popular propaganda put out by Franco."

"Toadying?" That's a good word. A hell of a lot better than this next one.

"Ernest Hemingway is just a tourist in Spain."

"Tourist"! Now that one pissed me off. But this last one is my favorite.

"Ernest Hemingway doesn't know his ass from his elbow."

Well, we all had days like that but Milt was wrong.

(He returns the letter.)

I will never forget the sacrifice of the men of the Abraham Lincoln Brigade. I knew what they were fighting for and I believed in them. That's why when Milt asked me to participate in their tenth anniversary,

I agreed, willingly. I have always supported those premature anti-fascists and I always will.

From Cuba, I sent what I hoped was a special recording to play at their reunion. It was recorded in Havana on an aluminum disc that cost $5.30. I hope you think it was worth it.

(He picks up the manuscript stage right and reads.)

The dead sleep cold in Spain tonight. Snow blows through the olive groves, sifting against the tree roots. Snow drifts over the mounds with the small headboards. (When there was time for headboards.) The olive trees are thin in the cold wind because their lower branches were once cut to cover tanks, and the dead sleep cold in the small hills above the Jarama River. It was cold that February when they died there and since then the dead have not noticed the changes of the seasons.

(He closes and holds the manuscript.)

It is several years now since the Lincoln Battalion held for four and a half months along the heights of the Jarama, and the first American dead have been a part of the earth of Spain for a long time now.

The dead sleep cold in Spain tonight and they will sleep cold all this winter as the earth sleeps with them...

But in the spring the rain will come to make the earth kind again. The wind will blow soft over the hills from the south. The black trees will come to life with small green leaves, and there will be blossoms on the trees along the Jarama River. This spring the dead will feel the earth beginning to live again.

For our dead are a part of the earth of Spain now and the earth of Spain can never die. Each winter it will seem to die and each spring it will come alive again. Our dead will live with it forever.

Just as the earth can never die, neither can those who have ever been free return to slavery. The peasants who work the earth where our dead lie know what these dead died for. There was time during the war for them to learn these things, and there is forever for them to remember them in.

Our dead live in the hearts and the minds of the Spanish peasants, of the Spanish workers, of all the good simple honest people who believed in and fought for the Spanish republic. And as long as all our dead live in the Spanish earth, and they will live as long as the earth lives, no system of tyranny ever will prevail in Spain.

The fascists may spread over the land, blasting their way with weight of metal brought from other countries. They may advance aided by traitors and by cowards. They may destroy cities and villages and try to hold the people in slavery. But you cannot hold any people in slavery.

The Spanish people will rise again as they have always risen before against tyranny.
The dead do not need to rise. They are a part of the earth now and the earth can never be conquered. For the earth endureth forever. It will outlive all systems of tyranny.

Those who have entered it honorably, and no men ever entered earth more honorably than those who died in Spain, already have achieved immortality.

(He returns the manuscript.)

On a mountain in Africa there is the dried and frozen carcass of a leopard. The soldiers of Spain, like this leopard, dared to go where no one else would go, they dared to look for freedom ... and they died for it. They died for this earth...for this Spanish Earth.

(Music: Conclusion of Jarama Valley)
(He kneels, kisses the earth, makes the sign of the cross, folds the cloth, stands, holds the earth to his chest and salutes.)

Salud!

(Fade to black)

**END of PART FOUR:
THE MAN-EATERS...**

...to be continued in part five: the death factory

Author's Notes

Lighting cues are minimal. Many venues will have no lighting facilities; however, when a traditional theatre is available, lighting will enhance the performance.

I encourage you to read Ernest Hemingway's *The Green Hills of Africa* and *For Whom the Bell Tolls*. Although fate kept me from going to Africa, I did get to Spain. What follows is a brief account of my visit to Madrid. The report is exactly as it was written for my website in 2002:

A few weeks ago, I traveled to Madrid and Pamplona to continue the research for my proposed play, *Hemingway On Stage: The Road To Freedom* (now called *The Hemingway Monologues*). While in Spain, I had the pleasure of meeting two of the finest gentlemen I have ever known, Stephen Drake-Jones and Thomas Entwistle. These men took me under their very erudite wings and revealed the secrets of Spain to me.

Steven Drake-Jones is the Chairman of the Wellington Society and one of the world's leading experts on the Duke of Wellington.
He is also an authority on The Prado, bullfighting, gourmet repasts, and all the haunts of Ernest Hemingway. I might also add that when I was attacked by Romanian gypsies in El Rastro the street market, his bravery and boldness helped me to fight them off. It

was a lesson well learned since I was attacked a second time when Stephen was not with me and, once again, using his technique, I scared the thieves away.

How wonderful it was to see the same paintings that Hemingway had viewed and enjoyed. Stephen had led art tours for many years and was able to fully explain the works of El Greco, Velazques and Goya. From elongated saints and vivid colours, through the inbred deformed face of Philip IV, to my favourites, "The Third of May 1808: The Mass Execution at Principe Pio" and the Black Paintings, possibly representative of Goya's nightmares and his abhorrence of a corrupt society.

Twelve bulls died for me (and a few thousand other people). Stephen has been an aficionado of the bullfights for almost thirty years and was able to explain every aspect of the spectacle. He was, in fact, able to anticipate every move of the President of the Corrida and would tell me seconds beforehand when the President was about to signal with a handkerchief for such moments as the exit of the picador. After the fight, I was treated to the less than appetite-stirring scene of the slaughter of the bulls. In a totally professional and speedy manner, they were dealt with prior to their journey to restaurants and the poor. Later, when I attended another bullfight by myself and occupied an excellent barrera seat, I found that I lost any aversion that I might have had to the spectacle and, by the end of the evening, was cheering and clapping with the Madrilenos.

Stephen also showed me Hemingway's Madrid. As I looked up at the impressive height of the Telefonica building, I could almost imagine Hemingway at the top writing, "They are bombing Madrid. I can see the

German planes and ... On we went. "Chicote's with the famous knocking door of the prostitutes, the Valencia sherry bar where stories were gained with the price of a bottle, Botin's famous suckling pig, to the headquarters of Franco's infamous secret police ... all these and many more turned Madrid and the Gran via into a museum of the Spanish Civil War. Finally, he introduced me to Tom.

Thomas Entwistle is considered to be the leading authority on the battlefields of the Spanish Civil War and it was with great pleasure that I marched up Suicide Hill with him, stood in the actual trenches and caves of the war and even found a few pieces of shrapnel. Tom showed me where one member of the Abraham Lincoln Brigade had his ashes spread as I began to understand the depth of this great fight for freedom.

Tom is the man who arranged the reunions of the ALB and reunited them years later to commemorate their part in the Spanish Civil War. Today, the battlefields are in danger of being overrun by developers with no sense of history. Is there any way we can help?
In the meantime, Charlie Nesser (deceased) of the Lincoln Brigade is reputed to have written a ply about his experiences in Spain. Hopefully, Tom and I can track it down and arrange for some form of presentation in the future.

Should you plan to visit Spain, I can think of no better guides than Stephen and Tom. They have both helped me immeasurably and I believe that *Hemingway On Stage* will be much better because of their contribution. Research is on target and I expect to have a completed script early in the new year. Slides and soundtracks will be created while I block and memorize for a workshop in June. After the workshop, I expect to be in good shape to debut the play at The Hemingway Days Festival in Key West.

(Please see the Tom Entwistle page near the end of this book in the In Memorium section)

The author in the Hemingway Room
of the Hotel Ambos Mundos in Havana, Cuba.

ABOUT THE AUTHOR
AND HIS WORK:

Brian Gordon Sinclair, author of *The Hemingway Monologues*, is a graduate of the National Theatre School of Canada and holds a Master of Arts degree in Theatre from the University of Denver. He also studied at the Royal Academy of Dramatic Arts in London, England, and at the National Film Board of Canada.

Mr. Sinclair's seven play series, *The Hemingway Monologues: An Epic Drama of Love, Genius and*

Eternity, has met with considerable critical acclaim, with the first five plays premiering at the Hemingway Days Festival in Key West, Florida. The sixth play, *Sunset* (originally titled, *In Deadly Ernest*), was commissioned by Museo Hemingway/Finca Vigia and had its world premiere at the Hemingway Colloquium in Havana, Cuba.

The playwright is a dual citizen of Canada and Ireland. His other works include *Easter Rising: The Last Words of Patrick Pearse*, a recreation of the dramatic days in Dublin during the 1916 struggle for Irish freedom. This play is available as an audio book. He is also the co-author of *The Homerun Kid: The True Story of Ernest Hemingway's Baseball Team*.

A recipient of the Sir Tyrone Guthrie Award for Acting at the Stratford Shakespeare Festival in Ontario, Mr. Sinclair has also received Awards of Distinction from Museo Hemingway and the University of Holguin in Cuba. He has performed in Canada, Cuba, Denmark, England, Norway, Holland, Poland, Spain, the USA and at the Moscow Art Theatre in Russia.

The Hemingway Monologues started in 2003 with *Part One: Sunrise*, where Mr. Sinclair's utterly convincing and evocative portrayal of Ernest Hemingway – as he fished for trout in Michigan, fell in and out of love, survived major shell wounds in Italy toward the end of World War One, then met and fell in love with a Red Cross nurse – had the Key West audiences, during the devastating final death scene, reduced to tears ... albeit, preceded by many lighter and humorous moments. The following descriptions are exactly as they appeared in the original opening night programs:

Part Two: The Lost Generation premiered in 2004 and tells of Hemingway's experiences in Petoskey, MI, his early work at the Toronto Daily Star newspaper and his marriage to Hadley Richardson. Hemingway and his wife move to Paris where the fledgling novelist meets Gertrude Stein, Ezra Pound, Pablo Picasso, F. Scott Fitzgerald and others. He is introduced to Spain and the pageantry of the bullfight and finally meets Pauline Pfeiffer, the woman who will steal him away from Hadley. From these experiences, Hemingway writes his first best-seller, *The Sun Also Rises*.

Part Three: Death in the Afternoon previewed before the Consul General of Spain in Toronto in 2005 prior to Key West. Hemingway attends the "Running of the Bulls" in Pamplona, learns of the life and death artistry of the corrida and dramatizes an actual bullfight. The play then moves to Key West and a brawl at Sloppy Joe's bar. Hemingway gets stranded in the Dry Tortugas, saves his son's life and plans a rebellion. The conclusion examines the destruction of the great hurricane of 1935.

Part Four: The Man-Eaters (This volume) premiered in Key West in 2006 in the presence of the Consul General of Canada. The play explores Hemingway's extra-marital relationship with Jane Mason, reenacts an African safari, explores dictatorship in Cuba and includes a fight with pirates. Hemingway then travels to Spain and the Spanish Civil War. As a war correspondent, he points out the atrocities of war and concludes with a stirring address that commemorates the Abraham Lincoln Brigade.

Part Five: The Death Factory premiered, after several delays, in Key West in 2009. From the joys of absinthe to the appeal of Ava Gardner, Ernest Hemingway turns to the exotic temptations of China and his third wife, Martha Gellhorn. Back in Cuba, he chases U-boats and tracks Nazi spies as a prelude to the European war and flying missions with the Royal Air Force. Whether commanding French freedom fighters or liberating the Ritz Hotel in Paris, Ernest manages to encounter Sylvia Beach, Marlene Dietrich, Pablo Picasso and Mary Welsh (later to become his fourth wife). While serving in "the death factory" that is World War Two, his emotional resources are strained when his first born son is taken prisoner by the Nazis.

Part Six: Sunset (originally *In Deadly Ernest*) premiered at the 11th International Colloquium Ernest Hemingway in June of 2011 at the Hotel Ambos Mundos in Havana, Cuba. The North American premiere occurred the following year in Key West. The play continues from the end of World War Two and concludes the chronological series. Earnest eagerly awaits the arrival of Mary Welsh and a new marriage. They deal with life in Cuba, Idaho and Italy as Mary runs the household at Finca Vigia, meets movie stars in Sun Valley and copes with her husband's infatuation in Venice. Ernest also shows his love for his middle son, Patrick, before moving on to publish *Across the River and Into the Trees* and *The Old Man and the Sea*. In Africa with Mary, Ernest is involved in two plane crashes that mark a gradual but certain deterioration in his health. After winning the Nobel Prize, he manages to continue writing in spite of the intrusions on his privacy. Eventually, a series of losses, including his beloved Finca Vigia, leads him to the Mayo Clinic and, finally, his demise.

Part Seven: Hemingway's HOT Havana is a special stand-alone edition. It is not part of the preceding six part chronological series. *Hemingway's HOT Havana* is a bold, rousing adventure tale brought to life by author, director and master story-teller, Brian Gordon Sinclair. It includes the following stories as excerpts from the original six plays and rearranged into a unique entertainment: life and crime in Havana ... writing tips for Arnold Samuelson ... Jane Mason ... baseball ... Ava Gardner...fishing the great blue river ... El Floridita ... the pirates of Havana Harbour ... shark attack ... lions, bears and banderillas...drinking with Hemingway ... German U-boats ... the Nobel Prize ... the death of Black Dog and Machakos ... and a shocking end. The show was originally performed, rough-hewn, in Havana on the rooftop of the former El Pacifico restaurant in 2005 during the precise moment of a total eclipse.

PHOTO GALLERY

At the African Lion Safari in Cambridge, Ontario, Canada

The author grapples with a vicious man-eater.

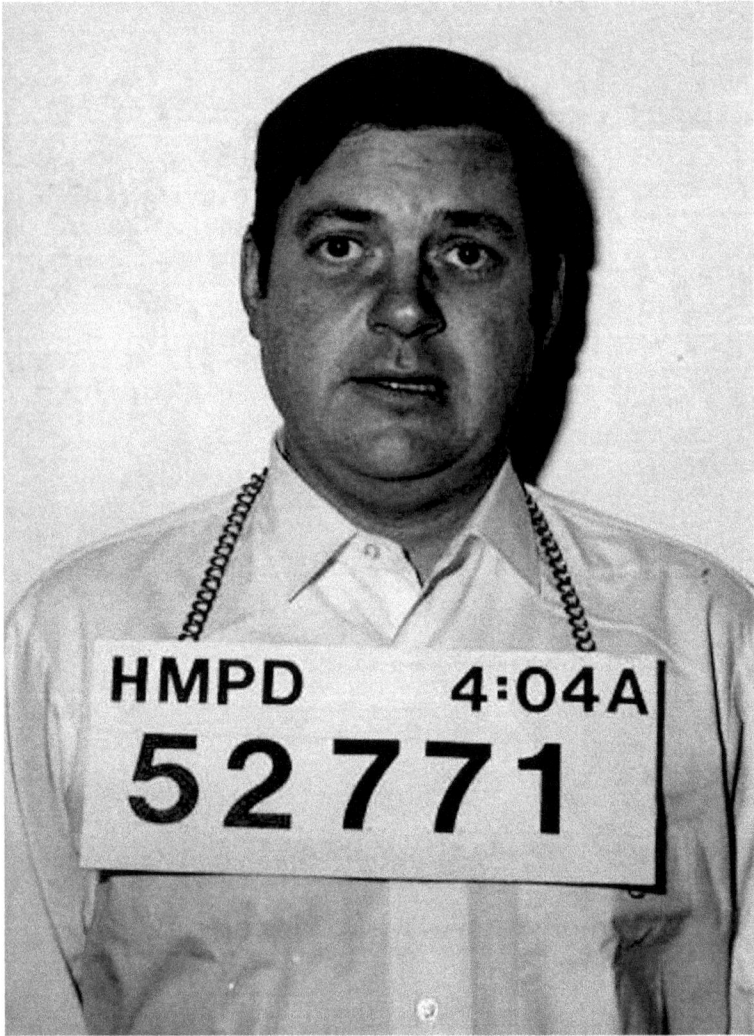

Earlier days 1980

Performing at the University of Denver, Colorado

Earlier Days 1997

As Theo Van Gogh in *Vincent*

Earlier Days 1999

Ready for a performance of *Love Letters*

Earlier Days

Standard publicity photo for theatrical agents.

With moustache and wig for *Sunrise*.

Hemingway enjoys pork and beans and spaghetti in
Sunrise.

With visor as worn by Hemingway on his boat *Pilar*.

Ready for the Annual Exhibition Game and Holiday
Celebration

A musical moment at El Floridita, Havana.

At the entrance to Finca Vigia/Museo Hemingway
prior to the premiere of
Sunset, originally titled *In Deadly Ernest*.

Two friends sharing a drink at El Floridita.

The Pilar at Finca Vigia

This author was pleased to stand on the deck of the boat of that author.

Hemingway's favourite dogs are buried near the site
of the former tennis court and the current drydock
location of his boat Pilar.

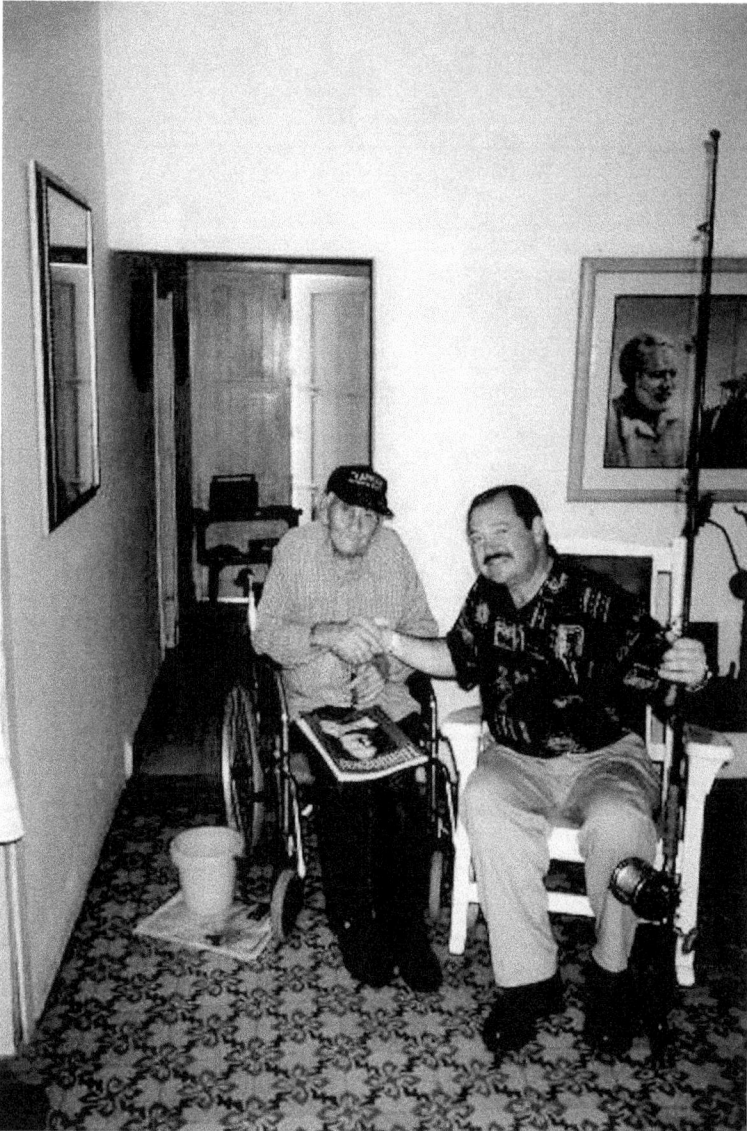

With Gregorio Fuentes in Cojimar, Cuba.
Gregorio passed away at the age of 104 but will
always be remembered as the "capitano" of
Hemingway's boat Pilar.

Our youngest Gigi All-Star. After watching him play in 2016, I believe he may become the new Homerun Kid.

The first delivery of Cubacan bats arrived at Finca Vigia in time for the 4ᵗʰ Annual Hemingway Exhibition Game and Holiday Event. The bats were donated by Bill Ryan, founder of Cubacan.

Original oil painting presented to Brian Gordon
Sinclair at Finca Vigia/Museo Hemingway, Dec. 3rd,
2015.

Cuban Artist: Elton Perez

Elisa Serrano, pictured at the concluding dinner of our 4th Holiday Event in San Francisco de Paula, is a brilliant Cuban painter and sculptor as well as a dear friend.

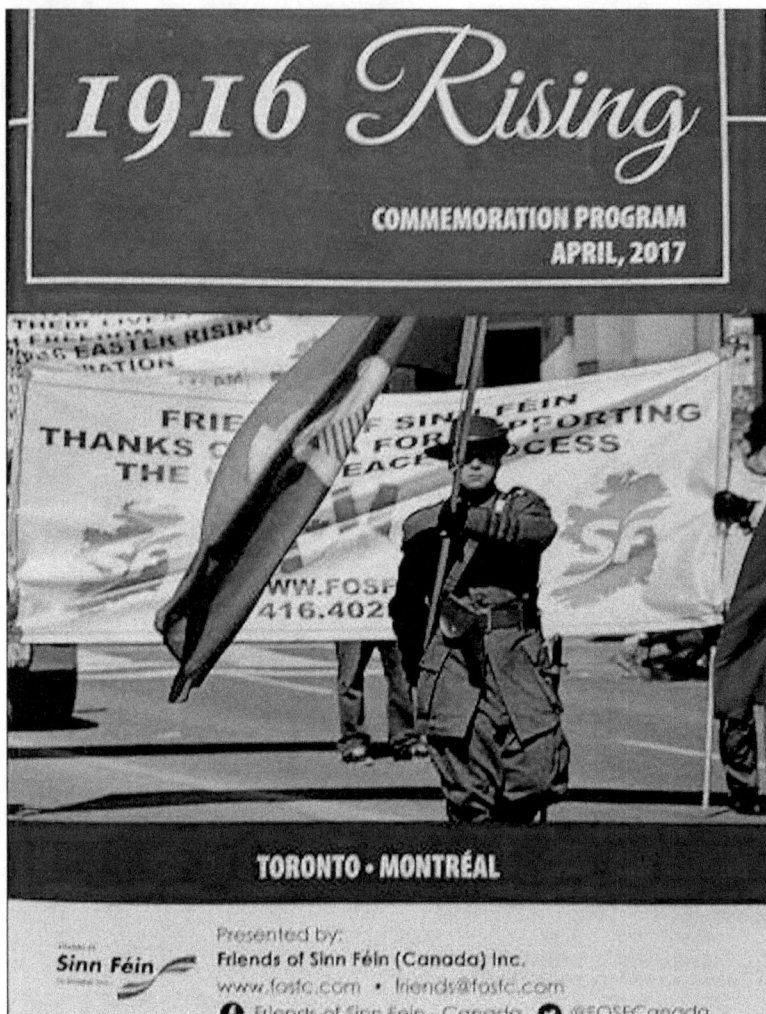

1916 Rising

COMMEMORATION PROGRAM
APRIL, 2017

EASTER RISING

FRIE... ...F SINN FEIN ...PPORTING
THANKS ... ...FOR...
THE ... ...EACE ...OCESS

WW.FOS...
416.402...

TORONTO • MONTRÉAL

Presented by:
Sinn Féin
Friends of Sinn Féin (Canada) Inc.
www.fosfc.com • friends@fosfc.com
Friends of Sinn Fein - Canada @FOSFCanada

The above uniform was created especially for me to wear in *Easter Rising: The Last Words of Patrick Pearse*. I recently donated it to Friends of Sinn Fein Canada and was pleased to see that it was featured in the St. Patrick's Day Parade.

Anyone interest in abstract art, will want to visit the
studio of Pavel Alvarez Mesa:
Calle 25 #1102 / 6 y 8, Vedado, Havana
Tel: 537 863 11 36Cell: 535 505 1975

Pavel specializes in the art of deformation which is
subjective, emotional and reflective of its time. The
above drawing, finally depicting a suicide, evolved
through the artist's emotions into a Hemingway
connection.

My upper body and deactivated shotgun are blended
with Hemingway's legs to create my version of his
iconic safari photo.

Photo by Charles Bryant

OTHER WORKS BY
BRIAN GORDON SINCLAIR

The Hemingway Monologues:
An Epic Drama of Love, Genius and Eternity

PART ONE

PART TWO

PART THREE

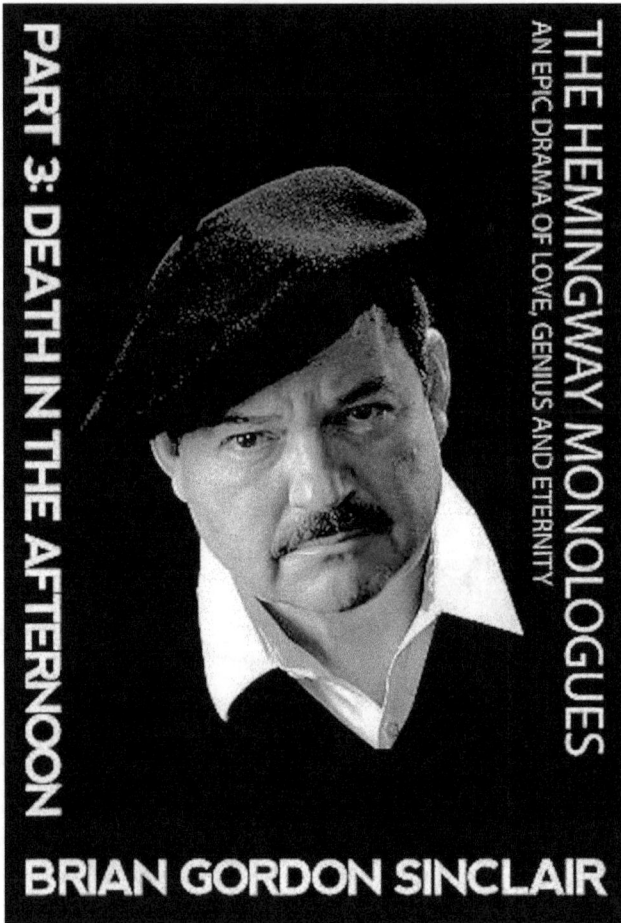

PART 3: DEATH IN THE AFTERNOON

THE HEMINGWAY MONOLOGUES
AN EPIC DRAMA OF LOVE, GENIUS AND ETERNITY

BRIAN GORDON SINCLAIR

The Hemingway Monologues: An Epic Drama of Love, Genius and Eternity is a seven-part dramatic series that reads like an intimate memoir. A fascinating blend of fact and fiction, the monologues reveal a tender, compassionate side of Hemingway that most people have never encountered. They can be enjoyed readily in performance or as a good, absorbing read. *Sunrise, The Lost Generation* and *Death in the Afternoon* are the first three plays of a series that traces Hemingway's chronology from birth to death. *The Hemingway Monologues* give an intimate insight into the circumstances which shaped the famed author's life and inspired him in his writing.

The first four volumes of the series, including this one, are now published. The remaining three volumes, to be published in order, will be available soon.

Hemingway's HOT Havana

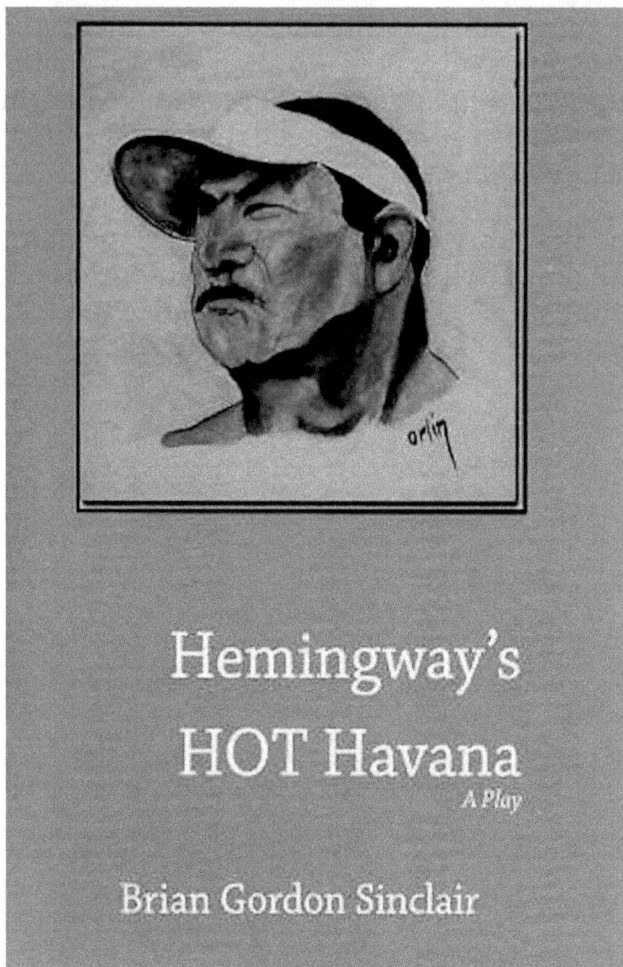

Soon to be revised, the original cover of *Hemingway's HOT Havana* displayed a composite drawing of Ernest Hemingway and Brian Gordon Sinclair.

Artwork by Robert Charles Orlin

Cuba Solidarity in Canada

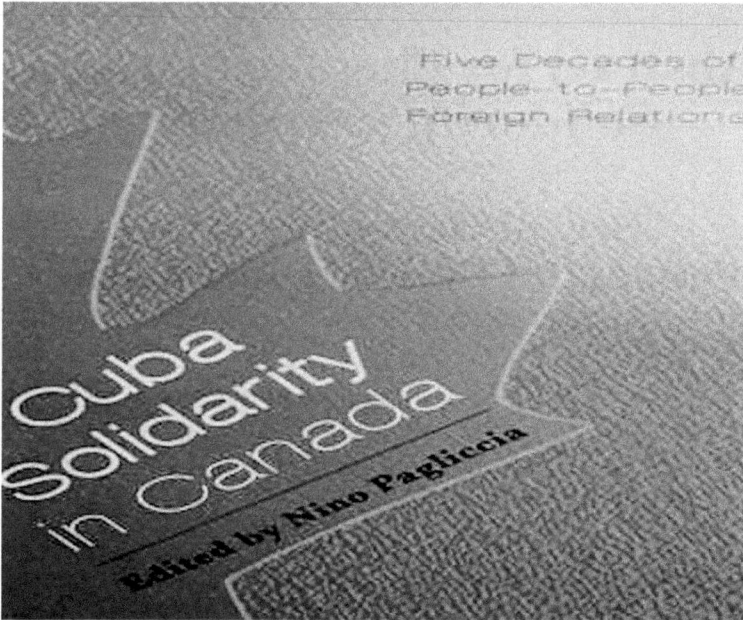

Cuba Solidarity in Canada – Five Decades of People-to-People Foreign Relations, is a collection of essays about the Canadian solidarity movement in support of Cuba over the course of 50 years. Throughout the different experiential stories, the notion of solidarity emerges as the common theme of people-to-people (non-governmental) links between Canada and Cuba. The book suggests a framework that informs the reader on the meaning, positive influence and potentially valuable role that solidarity can play in the relationship between peoples, indeed between nations. It also advances the possibility of a new paradigm of state-to-state foreign relations that is based on solidarity instead of ideological posture.

Included here is a final chapter by Brian Gordon Sinclair.

Abstract for Chapter 12, *Cuba Solidarity in Canada.*

"Ernest Hemingway: One Canadian's Doorway into Cuba."

I speak not of politics but of love. Ernest Hemingway opened a doorway that allowed me to discover the vibrant love of literature and people that is Cuba. He lived there for twenty years until forced out by America's fear of socialism. His spirit, however, is still there. I know that because when I meet the people of Cuba, as a writer and performer of Hemingway, I can feel it. His spirit exists in the people, in their hearts. Now he has moved into legend. In Havana, in Holguin and in Santiago, I have had the pleasure of sharing that legend. I have portrayed Hemingway at the 50th Anniversary of the meeting of Fidel Castro and Ernest Hemingway. They met at an international fishing tournament organized by Hemingway and where Fidel won the trophy for catching the most fish. I have appeared in Holguin at the Cuban 5 Colloquium while speaking in support of freedom and relishing the joy of a festival called Los Romerias de Mayo and I have appeared in Santiago de Cuba, sharing my work with students at the University of Oriente and participating in the astounding Festival of the Caribbean. In each case, my experience was intensely personal. In each case, Ernest Hemingway led me to and through an island that I did not know, to an island that now summons me to know more, much more.

                              - Brian Gordon Sinclair

Chapter 12 – Ernest Hemingway: One Canadian's Doorway into Cuba

(by Brian Gordon Sinclair 2014)

I must confess. I have taken a lover. Her name is Cuba and I am deeply and irrevocably in love with her. I did not choose to love her. When I arrived on her doorstep ten years ago, I was looking only for information and inspiration to help me write a single theatrical play about the life of Nobel Prize winning author, Ernest Hemingway. Little did I know that the beautiful, compassionate people of Cuba would open a doorway leading to a marriage of hearts and minds and souls. The offspring of that marriage would be an epic seven theatrical plays called *Hemingway On Stage: The Road to Freedom* and, even more epic, a lifetime of friendships. My experience, to now, has been limited to three major areas: Havana, Holguin, Santiago and their surrounding towns and villages. In each place, the people of Cuba warmed my heart and lifted my spirits.

From Havana, I went to the fishing village of Cojimar for the 50th Anniversary of the meeting of Fidel Castro and Ernest Hemingway. Cojimar, a short drive east of Havana, is the location that inspired Hemingway's novella, *The Old Man and the Sea*. The celebration was held in Pesca Deportiva Ernest Hemingway and was attended by members of the family of Gregorio Fuentes (First Mate of Hemingway's boat, *Pilar*) – daughter, granddaughter and grandson. My visit also included an interview by the press who wanted to know if I really believed that Fidel had caught the most fish in the 1960 Ernest Hemingway International Fishing Tournament. I told them that Hemingway had watched closely and that he had "an automatic built in bullshit detector and a damn fine pair of binoculars." He would never award the silver trophy to anyone who had cheated.

I also met several elderly fishermen who, as boys, had actually known Hemingway. One presented me with a small hand crafted mask of Ernest's face and told me about a fishing song that Ernest wrote. He is going to get me a copy. Afterwards, we traveled to the Hemingway monument near the Castillo where a wreath was laid to commemorate the anniversary. This monument, a bust of Ernest, was crafted from the bronze propellers donated by the fishermen of Cojimar. It was a gesture of love and respect. Finally, we went to *La Terraza* restaurant where special pictures of Hemingway and Castro had been newly hung. The management graciously served *mojitos* and *daiqiris* to everyone. I then returned to Havana, taking with me the grandson of Gregorio Fuentes, on his way to teach English to a class of waiting students and more than willing to give me a lesson or two on Cuba.

The next day was a magic day. I spoke as Ernest to the gathered crowd on the front balcony of *Finca Vigia*, now *Museo Hemingway*, directly in front of Ernest's writing room. For the first time in this humble actor's life, I was able to describe Ernest's home, *Finca Vigia* while, at the same time, pointing to the real building, the real saltwater swimming pool and the many mango trees as I described the creation of a children's baseball team named after Hemingway's son and called the Gigi All-stars.. A gentleman named Jorge still operates that team and "Hemingway On Stage" was very pleased to help arrange safety helmets for all the players.

At the end of the speech, which was offered in English with simultaneous translation by the fabulous Susana, I was able to present some computer accessories to the Director of Museo Hemingway as well as a modest donation raised for the ongoing work of the museum. In return, the Director of Havana Club distilleries presented me with a special edition rum: *Ron Vigia Reserva 18 Anos Produccion Limitada*. It bears the Hemingway *Finca Vigia* crest. You know, I've always wanted to try an eighteen-year-old rum but now that I've got it, it seems too precious. I don't want to break the seal. Perhaps, one day, you will join me in a very special toast.

I then made one more speech about dedicating the Nobel Prize Medal to the people of Cuba and the fishermen of Cojimar while depositing the medal at the El Cobre Sanctuary. As Ernest, I said a small, sincere prayer of gratitude which can be read in full in the Santiago section of this article. In the midst of the prayer, I swear, someone inside me said, "It's good to be home." Strange the things we sense but I do know that my voice cracked and I truly felt a presence. I concluded the prayer by crossing myself and saying "Amen". At that moment, every person in the audience, including the old fishermen and their wives, echoed me in a gentle but soul stirring "Amen". It was a true and holy moment. Just then, for one brief, glorious instant in time, Ernest Hemingway had come home. Later, the museum director, Ada, looked in my eyes and said, "Ernest is very happy today." The next day, because the appearance had been filmed, several million Cubans watched "Ernest Hemingway" pray for the people of Cuba on the cultural segment of the national news.

It is of tender, personal moments that I wish to speak and Holguin, Cuba provided many of these moments. When I performed at UNEAC, the headquarters for the Union of Artists and Writers, my audience consisted primarily of a wonderful group of Cuban students who were studying English. Also in the audience, uninvited, was a very large cockroach that chose the middle of one of my speeches to scuttle noisily across the floor. Since admission was complimentary, I couldn't very well throw him out so I continued. When I spoke of the Cuban flag and the love of Cuba, the students rose to their feet in applause. This old actor's heart was very proud at that moment. I hope the cockroach enjoyed it too.

I also remember, with great fondness, the night a dear friend, Elizabeth, joined me in an attempt to see a play celebrating the Cuban revolution and written by a Portuguese playwright, Leandro. Because of a technical problem, the performance was cancelled. Elizabeth, Leandro and I, along with a Colombian born Bostonian, headed for the cafes of Holguin's entertainment district. The conversation flowed and so did the time as we all entered into a lifetime of friendship but the hour was late and no traditional taxis were available, only bicycle taxis. With great revolutionary fervour, we leaped into three different bicycles. Each of us was transformed into an instant general. The race was on! I shouted the command, "Beat those bikes to the Hotel Pernik.!" The drivers huffed and puffed and strained their muscles and finally one pulled ahead by a few lengths and stopped in front of the hotel. Out stepped the winner. It was ... Ah, I am sorry but you know a gentleman never tells. I will tell you, however, that with the amount of laughter exuding from all the worthy combatants; no one was disappointed, least of all, the Cuban drivers.

On the last day of this visit, I traveled with a group to the attractive town of Baguanos. Here, the whole town came to greet us. Cheering people with flags and signs were at the intersections approaching the town and when we finally stepped off the bus, the town square was full. The band was there, military cadets were there and then six little drum majorettes marched forth and performed their tiny-perfect, precision routine. When they finished, the anthem played and they all stood very still at attention, radiant in their youth. It was then that it must have rained. How else could you explain the moisture rolling down my cheek?

Later, after visiting a street market, an art display and a cooking school (with lots of samples), we entered the town hall where we were entertained with music, song and poetry. There, I spoke as Ernest Hemingway. I told them that I had been out of Cuba at the moment of the revolution but that when I returned, I kissed the Cuban flag and stated that I believed in the absolute necessity of the Cuban revolution. I said that the photographers, at the time, did not manage to get a photo but today, because of the *milagro*, the miracle of theatre, I would be able to pose, kissing the flag, for photos. I then said that this day was different. I said, "Today, I kiss the Cuban flag because I believe in the absolute necessity of the freedom of the Cuban Five." I kissed the flag in honour of the Cubans imprisoned in America, held the pose briefly for photos and concluded by saluting and exclaiming, "Viva Hemingway, Viva Cuba, Viva los Cinco Heroes!" Would it be a surprise to say that the reaction was exceedingly positive?

Every arrival in Cuba feels like a spiritual return to a home where that special part of you has been too long away. My next visit to Holguin was like that, a lot like that. I was there, ostensibly to perform for the 20th Che Guevara Brigade, a band of adventurous Canadians of all ages determined to experience the real Cuba. After the show, there was a deluge of questions: "What Hemingway books can I read? How do I start writing? How do I learn to speak in front of an audience?" Each question meant that a curiosity had been aroused. They also told me that, in my play, *Hemingway's HOT*

Havana, I had demonstrated a very special love for Cuba, a love which they too hoped to share. If you have ever wondered about the mandate of Hemingway On Stage, the reaction of the Brigade demonstrates that mandate precisely.

A second show was for Los Romerias de Mayo (the pilgrimages of May). This cultural festival celebrates the founding of Holguin and, over the years, has become both national and international. It all started with a parade. God, I love a parade.

They marched into the city square, heads held high, through hundreds if not thousands of spectators, cheering, mesmerized by the pageantry. In the presentation area, a choir of white shirted singers stopped to sing. Beethoven's "Ode to Joy" rose, not from their throats, but from their hearts. Silvered paper rained from a balcony and we felt the joy enter our hearts in that special, shivering kind of way. We were transported.

Next, a hoard of Harleys roared central, (sorry, can't change this figurative choice) beautifully restored with flags flying in the morning air ... then the band, red shirts stepping out, brass instruments shining, gleaming in the sun ... followed by beautiful elegant girls, child and teen, draped in the flamenco finery of passionately graceful dance...vintage cars, trucks loaded with workers, revelers, all celebrating this day of joy ... and bringing joy to those, like me, who watched, spellbound.

The audience for my second performance also consisted of many Spanish students of English. They were an exceptional audience, responsive and attentive. I knew their English was good because I could actually see the comprehension in their eyes. They smiled, they listened and some cried. You see, when you mix love and death, love of Cuba and the death of Ernest

Hemingway, some people will be moved to tears. Later, in conversation, these students displayed a knowledge and an awareness of Hemingway that I can only wish existed in North America. They were warm, they were loving and they were smart. They said I touched their hearts. Truth is, they touched mine.

Santiago de Cuba is hot in every way, temperature, music, art and emotion. Like no other city, it arouses passion. It is also home to Roberto and Juan.

Roberto is a barber, a brilliant barber who cuts my hair in the old-fashioned way, with great passion. He massages my scalp, cleans and tightens the pores of my face and carefully trims the hair of both beard and head. Like any proud artist, he surveys the result of his work and pronounces me acceptable to walk on stage and perform. Roberto likes to cut the hair of "Ernest Hemingway". He is just as happy to cut my hair. He is proud; he is a master of his craft and he knows that true artists have great respect for each other. That's the way it is in Santiago de Cuba.

Juan is a special man. He knows everyone in Santiago and he likes to make things happen. Sometimes, however, things happen to him, like Hurricane Sandy. When Sandy hit Santiago, Juan and his family were at home. Outside, the winds of destruction roared and pounded. Have you ever heard the thunder of tanks in the midst of war, rumbling, shaking the very firmament? This was Santiago. This was Sandy. All Juan could do was to lie in bed, desperately grasping the sides, staring at the ceiling and praying that it would not collapse. His wife was curled up, locked in a ball, shaking and unable to talk. His daughter, elsewhere, listened fearfully to the sound of other roofs being blown away and watched, a strange smile frozen on her face, as her own roof lifted ominously in the violent air. She could not speak, only smile because, as she said later, she was "scared to death". In another room was Juan's son. Like all eleven-year-old boys he had his own reaction to the storm. He slept through it all, totally oblivious to the raging outside world. Juan and his family survived. Others did not.

It was Juan who first took me to El Cobre. We climbed the hill outside the city that passed the rugged, symbol-laden site of local ceremonies and rose to a view of an exquisite picture-perfect lake glowing blue and gold from the copper content, sparkling like a jewel in the heavens. Below was the church containing the El Cobre Sanctuary, beautifully restored for the visit of Pope Benedict. This was the church where Ernest Hemingway's Nobel Prize Medal was to reside, a gift to the people of Cuba.

Ernest Hemingway's Nobel Prize Medal was stolen from the El Cobre Sanctuary, located approximately twenty miles outside Santiago de Cuba, sometime in the 1980's. One version of the theft suggests that the thieves were not unknown to the local residents. When word reached Raul Castro, he reputedly issued an ultimatum, "Return the medal within seventy-two hours or face the consequences. I know who you are." Although the medal was returned, it was never again put on public display and remained, in hiding, under the care of the Archbishop of Santiago. Rarely has it been seen. The last person I know to have seen the medal was Ernest's granddaughter, Mariel Hemingway. On December 6, 2011, I was granted the rare privilege of viewing, holding and performing with the medal. A film crew from Mundo Latino captured the event for use, eventually, in a multi-part documentary about Hemingway in Cuba.

There is no proof that Hemingway ever accompanied the medal to Santiago; nevertheless, I have created a scene that depicts the arrival of the medal at the El Cobre Sanctuary. In discussing this scene with the staff of the Archbishop of Santiago, I explained that it was in the spirit of Hemingway but based on poetic or dramatic license. Soon a message arrived from the Archbishop's secretary, "We approve your 'license'."

What follows is a verbatim record of the scene as performed from memory and filmed in Santiago de Cuba using the actual Nobel Prize Medal of Ernest Hemingway: The text is from an original stage play written, directed and performed by the author of *Hemingway On Stage*:

HEMINGWAY:

After the war, I finally completed *The Old Man and the Sea* and I was almost killed in a plane crash in Africa. In 1954, for one or both of those things, I was awarded the Nobel Prize for Literature. This is a part of what I said:

(He picks up the speech and reads.)

"Writing at its best is a lonely life ... A true writer should always try for something that has never been done before ... Then sometimes, with great luck, he will succeed...It is because we have had such great writers in the past that a writer is driven far out, past where he can go, out to where no one can help him."

(He returns the speech.)

I dedicated my Nobel Prize Medal to the fishermen of Cojimar. Although I had told this story of an old man and his fish to the whole world, it is their story and they should share this medal.

A medal is worn close to the heart and my heart is in Cuba. The good people of Cuba have taken me into their hearts and caused me to live here longer than I have lived anywhere else. This is my true home.

Later, after a ceremony at the Modelo Brewery, I traveled with the medal to Santiago de Cuba and entered the church. There, in the El Cobre sanctuary, I knelt at the feet of the Patron Saint of Cuba and deposited the medal.

(He closes his eyes and prays.)

Silently, I prayed for the protection, the peace and the prosperity of the warm, friendly, generous people of Cuba.

(He opens his eyes.)

In Cuba, the people accepted me unconditionally. I could breathe and be happy. It is my clean, well lighted place.

(He crosses himself.)

Amen.

The preceding stories represent but a few of the special moments I have enjoyed in Cuba. How I wish there were time to tell you of all the others ... of the ghosts of the Sierra Maestra, the ghosts that are still there. I know this. I have been there. I have felt them, sensed them, still there on guard for freedom and change ... of Rosalba who cared for the dogs of the Hemingway estate and who died of cancer because she cared more for others ... of Adi who traveled to China to learn a new language to help her people ... of all the people who work at the Cuban Institute of Friendship with the Peoples, people like Kenia and Esperanza and Sandra and Amaury and Miriam, people who help because they love to help... and of the young teacher fresh with a Master's Degree who speaks of art and souls and rising spirits and I know that she is the future of Cuba, young and vibrant and in the process of being reborn in her search for truth ... These are the people of Cuba and they are all special.

Now, as I sit in the cold winter snows of Canada, I feel a soft, lonely ache in my heart. I need my love; I need my Cuba. Soon, Cuba, I will walk, once more, through the doors of your love and embrace you, for you are in my heart, a part of me, forever. Thank you, Ernest Hemingway and thank you, Cuba.

Brian Gordon Sinclair has travelled and performed extensively in Cuba in his capacity as a member of the Canada Cuba Friendship Association of Toronto, the Canadian Network on Cuba and as Patron of the Gigi All-Stars, the children's baseball team at Museo Hemingway/Finca Vigia.

Quotations used throughout the preceding article are from *The Hemingway Monologues* by Brian Gordon Sinclair.

Easter Rising: The Last Words of Patrick Pearse

Russia, Spain and Cuba provided three of the four greatest revolutionary dramas of the 20th Century. In 1916 Dublin, Ireland provided the fourth. It was called the Easter Rising and Easter 2016 will commemorate the 100th anniversary of the Rising. *Easter Rising: The Last Words of Patrick Pearse* is a recreation of the original event as told by the commander of the Rebel forces. A new edition, including an audio book version, is now available.

EASTER RISING
The Last Words of Patrick Pearse

A full length play for one actor. Written and produced by Brian Gordon Sinclair, a proud dual citizen of Ireland and Canada.

Easter Rising is a dramatic minute-by-minute account of the uprising, as told from a viewpoint in and around the General Post Office which functioned as rebel headquarters during the week of the siege.

O'Connell Street in flames

A theatrical tour de force, Easter Rising burns with the intensity of a city in flames.

The 1916 Irish Easter uprising was the first successful revolution in 20th century Europe. A pitiful band of revolutionaries, though scorned by most of their fellow Irishmen, were convinced that through their defeat and deaths they would arouse the Irish people to a victorious fight for independence. Amazingly, they were right, and out of the Easter Rising came a resurgence of the Irish nationalism which led ultimately in Irish independence.

Pierre Piety of Glasnevin Cemetery
Dublin, Ireland

Original costume design created for Easter Rising
by
F. Glenn Thompson, Artist/Historian, Dublin, Ireland

Constructed by Mary Logan, Stratford Festival, Canada

The Homerun Kid:

The True Story of Ernest Hemingway's Baseball Team

THE HOMERUN KID is a brilliant memoir, told with genuine childhood innocence!

A heart-warming tribute to Ernest Hemingway. You can feel a child's love for his hero permeating every memory, every word.

THE HOMERUN KID is more than a book of children's stories. It is a valuable addition to the history of Ernest Hemingway and offers a vivid, eye-witness account to scholars and aficionados.

THE HOMERUN KID should be read to young people in every library and classroom in the world!

THE ART OF STORYTELLING AT ITS FINEST! From the true stories of Cayuco "Jonronero" the Homerun Kid

Translation by Susana Hurlich
Adapted and edited by Brian Gordon Sinclair

$14.98

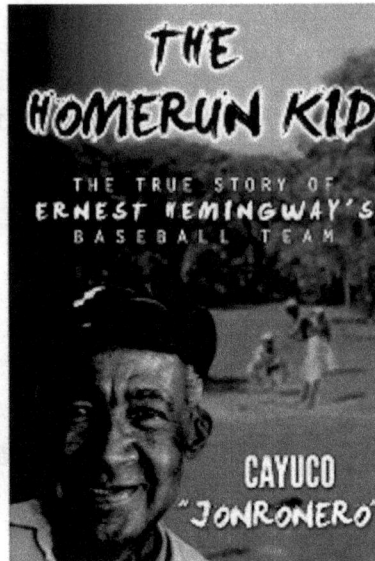

Adapted and Edited by Brian Gordon Sinclair
from the original stories of
Oscar Blas Fernandez Mesa.
Translation by Susana Hurlich.

Oscar Blas Fernandez Mesa passed away on Dec. 28, 2016 in his age 87th year. The book of his memories is now available for your reading pleasure. Please see the In Memorium section near the back of this book.

SPECIAL
INVITATION:

ANNUAL EXHIBITION GAME
AND HOLIDAY CELEBRATION

Estrellas de Guigui / Gigi All-Stars

HISTORY:

In the 1940's, a children's baseball team was formed to provide an activity for Ernest Hemingway's sons when they visited their father. It was named after Ernest's youngest son Gregory, also known as Gig and

Gigi. During this time, Hemingway provided uniforms, equipment and drove the kids anyplace they could arrange a game. At Christmas, the children were invited to Finca Vigia (Lookout Farm), the Hemingway estate, where Ernest would tell stories to the children and give each one a present.

Approximately, seven years ago, The Director of Museo Hemingway (Ada Rosa Alfonso Rosales) and Oscar "Cayuco" – the Homerun Kid – Blas, the 86 year old surviving member of the original team, decided to revive the team known as the Estrellas de Guigui/the Gigi All-Stars. It has been my pleasure to assist with that revival. In December of 2013 (helped by Papa Wally Collins of the Hemingway Lookalike Society), I not only had the privilege of arranging uniforms and equipment for the team but I also revived the storytelling tradition along with the presentation of a gift to each child. Each player received a card containing one dollar and a copy of the book from which the story was taken. Naturally, the book and story vary from year to year. So far, the children have received copies of *The Hemingway Monologues: Part One-Sunrise, Part Two-The Lost Generation, The Pirate Night before Christmas* and *The Homerun Kid*. Many more books are to come.

As Patron of the Gigi All-Stars, I invite you to join us for the Annual Exhibition Game and Holiday Celebration. The event is held yearly at Museo Hemingway in San Francisco de Paula on the outskirts of Havana and takes place on the first Saturday of December. Admission to the event is complimentary. Hemingway, baseball, literature, children and Christmas – the perfect combination.

- Brian Gordon Sinclair
Patron

QUESTIONS?

Contact Hemingway On Stage

sinclair4814@rogers.com
www.briangordonsinclair.com

P.O. Box 337
Alliston, ON, Canada L9R 1V6

IN MEMORIUM

OSCAR BLAS FERNANDEZ MESA
"CAYUCO JONRONERO"
THE HOMERUN KID

Oscar Blas Fernandez Mesa.
Known to his friends as "Cayuco", he was the original "Homerun Kid".

After years of playing for and caring for Ernest Hemingway's baseball team, Cayuco left us on December 28, 2016

I miss him, now and forever.

What follows is a speech that will be delivered in my name by our dear friend Susana Hurlich at the 2017 International Hemingway Colloquium in Havana, Cuba:

CAYUCO TRIBUTE

by BRIAN GORDON SINCLAIR

How sad I am that I cannot be here in person today to speak of my dear friend, Cayuco "Jonronero." Please, allow me to use some of the words we shared in our book. I thank our dear friend and partner, Susana Hurlich, for speaking these words on my behalf.

In 1940 Ernest Hemingway arrived in Cayuco's Heart. In 2015, Cayuco arrived in my heart. After seeing me perform as Hemingway at the 14th International Hemingway Colloquium, he asked if I could help him prepare a book of his baseball memories - memories of his friends and of Ernest Hemingway.

In adapting the stories of Cayuco "Jonronero", I attempted to enter into his mind and to feel as he felt. The stories, told from the viewpoint of a child through the luxury of historical perspective, appeared simple but were rich in the complexity of compassion. I knew that was true when the writing and reading of the stories brought tears in the most positive of ways. The lessons were valid in the 1940's and are no less valid today. Thank you Cayuco for allowing me to share your life. The experience has been both heart-warming and richly rewarding.

Cayuco showed us a kinder, warmer, more compassionate Hemingway than we had known. He was able to do this because he was kind. He was warm. He was compassionate. In telling his stories, I became kinder, warmer, more compassionate. Some people give a name to these qualities. That name is love. Thank you Cayuco for instilling that love in me. For the rest of my life, I will share that love with everyone I meet and in sharing that love, I will be sharing you. And they, in turn, will share your love. You and your love will go on and on and that love will live forever. Thank you Cayuco and welcome to eternity.

Finally, I will leave you with a short poem which I included in our book:

A golden Smile
A Friend's Embrace
Warm
Gentle
Thoughts
For You
In Dreams
Your Dreams
My Dreams
All Dreams
Sharing
Caring
Moving
Onwards
Ever
Remembering
Forever
Grateful

How proud I am to have worked on this book with you. How proud I am to have been your friend. Please know that my friendship will be with you and your family forever. Maria Luisa, children, grandchildren, Estela – I love you, now and forever.

\- Brian Gordon Sinclair
Patron
Estrellas de Guigui

Brian Gordon Sinclair

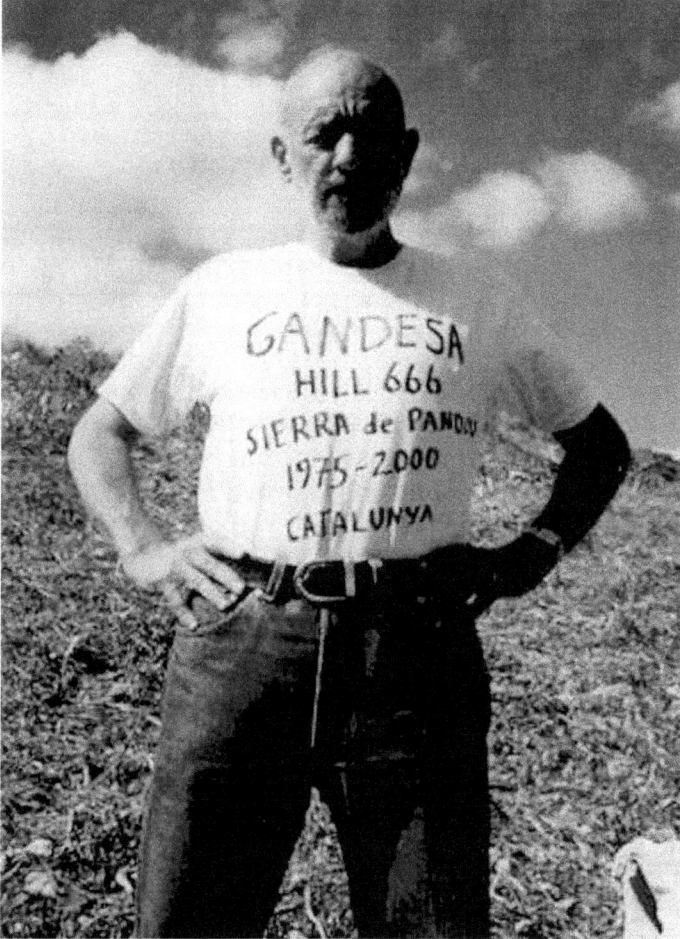

Thomas Entwistle

Tom passed away in a hospice in Guadarama near Madrid, Spain on Dec. 28, 2003.

(Photo courtesy of John C. Howell)

Website Entry, January 17, 2004.

I was devastated to learn of the death of Tom Entwistle. My time with him was precious and I miss him terribly. How often I looked forward to seeing him again and how often I dreamed of showing him my completed Hemingway play. The play has turned into a vast epic and will require about six separate plays before it is completed. The Spanish Civil War section will probably be in play number four and it will contain moments discussed with and inspired by Tom. That particular play will, in fact, be dedicated to Tom for he was the guardian of the battlefields, the living chronicle of the sights, the sounds, and the heroism that was the Lincoln Brigade. Who, oh, who will carry on the legacy? I only pray that my work will do justice to Tom and to all that he stood tall for. Whenever and wherever you toast him, I raise my glass in unison. God speed and God bless, Tom.

www.briangordonsinclair.com

ENRIQUE CIRULES
AUTHOR
1938 - 2016

Enrique Cirules was awarded many literary prizes including the Casa de las Americas and the Literary Critics Award. His numerous works include *The Mafia in Havana, The Secret Life of Meyer Lansky in Cuba, A Conversation with the Last American* and *The Unknown Hemingway.*

Enrique was a warm, gentle man. He was also a passionate man, passionate about writing and passionate about truth. I first met him at a Hemingway Colloquium at the Hotel Ambos Mundos in Havana, Cuba where I was performing the final play of *The Hemingway Monologues*. Enrique was elegant. He never walked; he glided – tall,

perfectly dressed and perfectly composed. He was a presence. Because of his interest in Hemingway, we became friends. Each year that friendship deepened as he joined me at my annual holiday event at Museo Hemingway and I joined him in conversations about his latest book, *The Unknown Hemingway*. I will never forget the hours spent tracing the maps of Hemingway's submarine/Nazi search throughout the Camaguey Archipelago. We sat at a marble table on the patio of Havana's Hotel Presidente examining a map of the archipelago which I had brought. Enrique pointed out that the map was limited and began drawing an extension of Hemingway's route which, in indelible black ink, ran right off the map and onto the marble tabletop. Someday I will return and see if the marks are still there. There are other marks though. The marks he left on my heart and the hearts of others. Rest in peace, my friend.

FIDEL
August 13, 1926 - November 25, 2016

    The equal rights of all citizens to health, education, work, food, security, culture, science and wellbeing – that is, the same rights we proclaimed when we began our struggle, in addition to those which emerge from our dreams of justice and equality for all inhabitants of our world – is what I wish for all.

    I think that a man should not live beyond the age when he begins to deteriorate, when the flame that lighted the brightest moment of his life has weakened.

Fidel Alejandro Castro Ruz

THE DEAD IN SPAIN

1936 – 1939

In this presentation of *The Man-Eaters,* I humbly honored the valiant who died, fighting against fascism during the Spanish Civil War. How proud I was to stand and salute in front of the images of those who truly fought. Clutched to my chest, was the Spanish Earth for which they fought. As the stage darkened, the flag of the Republic rose majestically in the wind while the music of Jarama Valley grew throughout the auditorium bringing the audience to a thunderous ovation.

"...they dared to look for freedom ... and they died for it."

Coming soon!

PART FIVE
OF THE
HEMINGWAY
MONOLOGUES:

THE DEATH FACTORY

NewAtlantianLibrary.com
or AbsolutelyAmazingEbooks.com
or AA-eBooks.com

The New
Atlantian Library

www.ingramcontent.com/pod-product-compliance
Lightning Source LLC
Chambersburg PA
CBHW052112090426
42741CB00009B/1774